# How to Your Second Life, First

## The Shortcuts You Don't Need

*The Buddha famously said,
we have two lives to live. The second life
begins when we realise we only have one.*

SIMON LESLIE

# CONTENTS

| | | |
|---|---|---|
| **Prelude** | | 5 |
| **Introduction** | | 11 |
| | | |
| **Chapter One:** | The End. | 17 |
| **Chapter Two:** | My Ten Rules for Success. | 23 |
| **Chapter Three:** | Where have you got to in life? | 33 |
| **Chapter Four:** | Life is all about the stories you create. | 37 |
| **Chapter Five:** | Mind the way you speak, act, and think. | 39 |
| **Chapter Six:** | Man plans and God laughs | 43 |
| **Chapter Seven:** | Good Energy | 45 |
| **Chapter Eight:** | Who Do You See in the Mirror? | 49 |
| | | |
| **Final thoughts** | | 53 |
| **About the author** | | 63 |

# PRELUDE

Life isn't meant to be lived on autopilot. Yet, you probably are. You find yourself going through the motions without forward movement, trading your dreams for the safety of a job (that you possibly hate), postponing your deepest aspirations for a mythical "someday." We tell ourselves, "Someday I'll pursue that passion. Someday I'll start that business. Someday I'll write that book." But here's the truth: Someday Isle is a destination most never reach. This book is your wake-up call. It will ask you questions you probably don't have the answers to yet, but it will prompt you to think about what you were put here for.

It's time to stop making excuses and start living your second life now. You've completed your education and gone through enough phases; it's time to figure out who you really are and where you are on your timeline for the life you are about to lead. It is crucial to have an opinion, to stand for something. You need to get away from the crowds and discover who you really are and what your purpose is.

These aren't just philosophical statements – they're the foundation of a life well-lived.

Living your best life means maximising your potential and striving to achieve the highest quality of life possible. It means being true to yourself and your values while making choices that align with your personal goals and aspirations. It's about being intentional in the way you live and making the most of the time you have.

It encompasses elements of physical, emotional, spiritual, and financial well-being. It means taking care of yourself and your health, nourishing your relationships, pursuing your passions and interests, and finding a sense of purpose and fulfilment in your life.

This book is a brain dump of my ideas about living your best life now or, at least, beginning that process. It doesn't matter if it's the first, second, or fiftieth iteration. We only get one go at this, and sometimes we mess it up. This is what I learned, how I got some things right, got a lot wrong, found success, and learned from my failures. Your life is not like a jigsaw; it's doesn't end with a perfect picture, where you make up a small piece of it. It's all about progress and staying aware of the strides you are making all the time.

Here's a spoiler alert – no matter what you achieve, something will always be missing; it's your job to figure out what or who you need to complete you in each of the phases you will go through. I do not care what anyone tells you; you will never be satisfied. There will always be people who are richer, more successful, happier and more established than you. And at times you will scratch your head and ask yourself, what's this all about?

### To all the people in my life

I wrote this book for you, to help you really think about what is important right now. For you to create a blueprint of the life you love. It's based on my mistakes, my learnings, and what I did to ensure you experienced the best that life has to offer. In my pursuit of this, I was not always present; I sacrificed much on my journey. You may or may not want to make those sacrifices as well, yet I believe there is a way to navigate the nonsense. I want you to keep this book by your side; there will be a scenario for whatever life throws at you, so you are ready.

This book will help you ask better questions, challenge your thinking, and understand that, no matter how dark the path, there is a light at the end. It will all be okay in the end; if it's not okay, it's not the end. (My grandma.)

People will always ask you silly questions, like, "Are you happy?"

Consider how you can rephrase the question; never answer silly questions. Challenge them back–turn the question around. Do you mean, "What makes me happy?" or "Am I happy with what I have achieved?" These are much more useful and powerful questions. If there is only one thing you take from this book, let it be this: don't worry about what people think or say about you. Other people's thoughts and opinions won't pay your bills, and they really don't matter at all.

This is your world, and only your opinion of yourself matters. Don't be mean or unkind to yourself; you are not fat, ugly, mean-spirited, or anything else negative. Be as kind to yourself as you are to others.

Every amazing opportunity you seek will come gift-wrapped in problems. Unravel the problems to find your prize. At times, you might not feel like the brightest candle in the room, but be prepared to keep your light burning longer than anyone else's. Remember, one candle can light up many other people's candles.

Life is both simple and hard, and as humans, we often try to make it easier. It was never easy; nothing is easy. We also complicate what is simple to make ourselves feel better. It's not about how good you are; it's about how good you can be and who you can bring with you on the journey. You need to determine who you want around you. There is no easy route in this world; there is no life hack to success, so stop looking for shortcuts. It takes many hours to become good at anything. Learn something new every day; you can never know enough about yourself. Discover what makes you tick, what annoys you, and what inspires you. Don't ever worry about what you are not good at; you'll find people to handle those tasks. When you figure out what you are good at, focus on doing much more of that, and never stop learning.

Be proud of who you are and what your values are. Stand for something and stick to those beliefs until proven otherwise. Discard all the biases that social media peddles to you. Be kind. Be mindful of your thoughts; they will either create space or tension. Create more space; spend more time doing what makes **YOU** happy and think positively and creatively to find solutions. Don't waste time and energy dwelling on things you can't change.

This planet is full of people who think they know it all, yet very few actually do. Everyone has problems; don't ever wish for things to be easier—just find a way to be stronger. No one has a perfect life, and anyone you think has it all does not. Wanting things to be easy is the greatest threat to your progress.

Few things in life are certain. You know the day you were born, but we have no idea how many days are available to us from that day. Just make as many of them winning days, and life will turn out more than fine.

Never forget to tell people that you love them, always say thank you, and truly appreciate every day you have.

Finally, ensure you are adding value to everyone you meet. Help enough people get what they want, and your life will be truly magical. Do what makes you happy, not what you think the world expects of you.

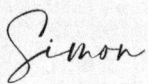

# INTRODUCTION

Most people write books based on societal norms, logic, and learning. My book is based on real experiences, real failures, really dark times, and plenty of good times. You need to understand the dark times to appreciate the light and how to shine it on yourself and everyone you meet. There is zero theory in this book. Every thought, every idea, is one I have lived out and mostly borrowed from something I heard somewhere. I learned very little from formal education; I used travel to influence my thinking. There is no bias from a programmed or over-educated brain. I am still trying to figure out where the mind is located, along with science. I have always been curious. I am happy to say that despite 56 years on this planet, I still know so little. There is so much more to learn. What I will share with you is what I did to accelerate my personal performance, improve my energy, and leave everyone you meet feeling warm and fuzzy about you. I will challenge your beliefs and the stories you tell yourself and show you how to find a way, even if you feel like you are at a dead end. It's about being comfortable with being lonely and alone in your own thoughts.

> ***Nothing needs to make sense.***
> ***Success is not logical. Magic exists in***
> ***psychology; it does not exist in physics.***
> ***Never ever let logic kill the magic.***

Life is not just what happens to us in this weird and wonderful world. It's the narrative, reactions, and stories we tell ourselves to justify it and make sense of our journey. Our existence is a blockbuster movie; we decide what part we play, and the better we narrate the script, the better our performance turns out. The sooner you master this, the sooner your existence improves.

Here's a thought: you may believe the plans you have will lead you to the life you want, but they won't. Lady luck, hard work, and the decisions you make in the moment will create the world you inhabit. Grand plans are great, but it's the bumps in the road, the failures, and the moments when things go awry that will shape who you become. The things that frustrate us often make us better. Ignore the noise that tells you what happiness and success should look like; it will only slow down or even defer your happiness. Do more of the things you dislike, and you will come to appreciate the benefits they bring you. Don't compete; instead, find a way to dominate. Rather than blaming your family or circumstances, create your own family and circumstances. No one will ever spend money on a ticket to your pity party.

Take authorship of your story. Listen to your worries and anxieties; they may keep you safe but are also sending you clues. Take your clues and cues from deep within you, not from a harsh outside world. You have all the answers—certainly not from the media, whether social or otherwise. Understand that your priorities will shift, and your focus is always changing. Change is healthy. You really need to get comfortable with being uncomfortable.

As a youngster, surround yourself with wisdom—grandparents, experienced souls, and grey-haired people—and when you reach 40, seek out youth and youthful ideas. Growing old is mandatory; growing up is still optional. Stay youthful and always be curious. Find people who have accomplished what you want to achieve, befriend and learn from them. Find a running mate and keep each other on course. Those are the three groups that will help you enjoy the race.

Play your best, practice, improve, and refine your skills; use positive language. Don't use limiting language. You are not ***insert the word*** that you use frequently (e.g., depressed, sad, anxious) and think about too much. The truth is this: you are simply not quite ready, unfinished, a masterpiece in progress. You may not be noticing all the progress you are making. Understanding progress will be one of your superpowers. Reflect on how much you are improving; look for the clues. You write better emails, have better conversations, and are more confident in various situations. Be a world-class noticer. Acknowledge the differences, even if they seem small. Noticing how you are growing will help you grow. As you get better, the growth is so much smaller and sometimes hard to notice.

It's my greatest desire that this book helps you improve your life. It offers ideas to see the world through a different lens and provides you with an edge over your competition. It will help you accelerate your vision of success so you can realise your greatest wishes and ambitions. Right now, the most significant investments you can make are in yourself. You are your greatest asset. There is no shortage of opportunities, there is however a shortage of determination and conviction.

Not everything is about money; not everything is about brands or shiny objects. Sometimes, the smell of bread, coffee, and flowers, as well as witnessing sunrises and sunsets in both nearby and faraway places, is what truly matters. It's about making others feel special, not just yourself, and leaving everyone you meet glad to have made your acquaintance. Money is there to be used, not as a measure of your worth. Be kind, first and last. Drive is not just about working long hours; it's about appreciating sleep. It's about recharging, like your car, and finding time to learn, grow, and walk every day. Go back to nature, ground yourself, and climb mountains. Find time to enjoy your own company.

At 17, I dreamed of being a millionaire; by 19, I had my house repossessed and my car snatched back, ending up in the spare bedroom at my parents' home. I learned early that failure is the greatest teacher. By 40, I had everything a man could want: the family, the house, the car, and a successful business, yet I hated everything—especially myself. The journey of the last sixteen years has given me the foundation of this book. My hop, skip, and jump through the subjects of happiness, success, and peace of mind have led me to a place of confidence and self-awareness. I understand what I stand for and will not allow anyone else to derail me. No longer chained to a desk, I now appreciate the reflection in the mirror and aim to be an energy charger for everyone in my world, spreading motivation daily and helping young people find their passion, purpose, and the 'why' and 'what' of it all.

There are many thoughts in here; dip into the bits you need when you need them. I have contemplated various situations, and I believe many are covered. If not, just reach out and ask me.

***Your home is not a place; it's the people in your life. It's where others notice when you are not around.***

# CHAPTER ONE:
## The End.

What do you want the end to feel like?

As I write this, according to statistics, I might only have 19 summers left. That's not very long, so it's important to appreciate that I cannot waste too much time being sad. It feels like yesterday that I thought I had loads of time to meander through life, not worrying a jot. Life goes fast; please make sure you are using your time wisely.

I always start with the end and reverse engineer everything. So, I decided to write my own eulogy; this is a tribute to my life. It's slightly different from an obituary or a tombstone, which are more factual, and in the case of a tombstone, have limited space. On your tombstone, there is no room for how many houses, cars, or watches you had, nor for where you went on holiday or how many times you dined at Nobu. They only indicate when you were born and when you died, and whether anyone really liked you or who you left behind. In my talks, I refer to it as **The dash to the finish** because your whole life is summed up in a dash between two dates. Maybe one day someone will invent a QR code that, when you hold your phone over a tombstone, plays a video of your life. Well, I hope someone does that for me. That is why I am living my best life; I want to live a blockbuster movie, not a forgettable sitcom. I want to be played by George Clooney, not end up as a Ricky Gervais character.

Life begins with smiles and ends in tears. How about rewriting that line and letting life end with smiles too? Make your end a celebration of the things you did, the people you helped, and the lives you impacted. The more you do for others, the better your life will become.

Yes, it's tongue-in-cheek, and there are still things I have yet to achieve, but I will.

***Simon Leslie was born in Cardiff, South Wales.*** He was a surprise to himself and his parents that this annoying kid, who had no idea what he wanted out of life, would go on to achieve so much— so much more than he or anyone else expected. He flunked school but became a charming salesman. Yes, a simple door-to-door salesman who went on to build the world's biggest travel media company and dominate in many sectors. He found a way, even when there seemed to be none. No one had more scraps with failure.

He was an outspoken critic of nonsense—he truly believed that nothing needed to make sense. Simon had a passion for family, travel, cigars, and sports. He could often be found on a distant beach with a cigar in his gob or at a major sporting final. He was an adventure seeker who loved a challenge, pushing himself beyond his perceived limits. He completed marathons, a half Ironman, climbed Kilimanjaro, and even ran a double marathon across the Sahara. He jumped out of planes and was always raising money for charity. He helped many change their lives for the better, although he did upset some in the process. He was demanding, wanting people to deliver their full potential; he could often be heard saying, "No one knows how good they can be; it's my job to push them, kicking and screaming, to that place." He travelled extensively and visited over 100 countries. He redrew the map of Kigali after the genocide and was kidnapped in Lebanon. He was always there to listen and offer great advice. An author of four books, he wrote thousands of motivational poems (@themotivationalpoet). He was a big man with a kind and generous heart. He leaves behind four super-wise, kind, and caring sons and a wife who can finally sleep without his incessant snoring. He was happiest by the sea. His dream was to build a football club where everyone is valued and appreciated, which he viewed as beneficial for the fans, the players, and the sponsors; this was his greatest achievement. He pushed for changes to the game that made it better for younger players, taking the club from nowhere to somewhere and winning cups. He made Eastbourne Borough famous all over the world. A true lifelong learner, he was always listening to a podcast, an audiobook, or an inspirational speech. Simon wanted everyone to become a better version of themselves.

On many occasions when I give a talk, I tell a story about a man called Amazing.

This man called Amazing had been ridiculed all his life. At school, his friends would bully and tease him, saying, "Ooh, that's amazing work that is!" or "Oh, aren't you amazing, Amazing!" At work, it was a similar story; even during his children's wedding speeches, they would include how amazing a dad he had been. As he came to the end of his story, he said to his wife, "I ask you one thing: please don't put my name on my headstone." A few months later, he died, and his headstone read:

Here lies a beautiful husband of 36 years, a doting father to four wonderful kids and seven adoring grandkids. A pillar of the community and a kind, generous, loving human. A true gentleman who was a shoulder to cry on. He left everyone he met better than he found them.

One day, two old ladies were walking through the cemetery, and one turned to the other and said, "Look at that; that's amazing!"

Amazing story, right? No one even needs to know your name to leave a mark on this world. Leave your mark; leave everyone you meet better than you found them. Let them talk about you. Surprise and delight people. Understand what you want life to look and feel like. Always start with the end in mind and work backwards. Say what you can do and do what you say.

We have only one life; sometimes we need to have a breakdown or a breakthrough to realise this. The theme of this book is finding a second life without going through the pain. As I understand it, this means prioritising and actively pursuing the life that you truly want to live, rather than merely going through the motions of your current life. It means identifying your passions, goals, and aspirations, and making them a priority in your life. It's about taking action to create the life you want, rather than just dreaming about it and waiting for the "right" time to pursue it.

It's about embracing change, taking risks, and not being afraid of failure. It's about finding fulfilment and happiness in the present, rather than waiting for it in the future. It means being true to yourself and your values, rather than conforming to societal expectations or living a life that is not authentic to you. Test a few different ideas and be good at experimenting, don't just ask your family and friends for their opinion.

Living your second life first is about making the most of the time you have and creating a life that is meaningful and fulfilling. It's about taking control of your life and prioritising it, rather than living it passively or making excuses about why it can't be better now.

## *Do what you love, not what's expected.*

# CHAPTER TWO:
## My Ten Rules for Success.

### 1
**Be careful who you mix with.**

Oil doesn't mix with water, and it's important that your circle doesn't become your cage. If the people in your circle don't inspire you, then it's not a circle but a cage. Change them out regularly and spend as much time alone as you can; read, listen, watch, and observe others. Sit in street cafés and people-watch. Study the people you admire and consider why you like them. Find people who are just ahead of you, who have done what you want to do, and who are prepared to guide you on your journey. You want to meet famous people, spend time with them, listen to their podcasts, read their books, watch their videos, write to them, and then one day, when or if you meet them, you will have a connection with them and will ask great questions. I was inspired by Tim Grover, I read all his books, and watched his content. I gave a copy of my book to a friend who ended up giving it to John Terry, the then Chelsea captain. When Chelsea won the Premier League, he was quoted in the press as saying that book had helped them be Relentless. When I met Tim Grover, I told him that story. Since that day we have been good friends, and he has supported me in business and with my football team.

# 2
## Patience is the key.

The overnight success story is largely a myth. Real, lasting success is more akin to watching a tree grow than lighting a match. You can accelerate that process by spending time with the right people, as per Rule One. You must invest in yourself; don't wait for the lessons, as they will come thick and fast as you start to win. The critics will be out in force; listen to what they are saying, and then ignore the noise. They are there to give you feedback. Sometimes the feedback will be merited, and you will need to take note; at other times, it will be fit for the bin. Patience comes from the Latin word "pati," which means to suffer, so please understand there will be plenty of suffering along the way. Progress is a race with no finish line. Plant your seed now, water it, look after it and prune it, when it needs it.

# 3
## Don't buy into the labels.

I used to think I was wrong, but it turns out I wasn't. People will always have opinions about your actions and decisions—some may say you're doing great, while others may perceive it as a disaster. However, their perceptions are based on their own perspective, not yours. They don't have the full picture of what's going on in your mind or understand your vision. Instead of labelling things as good or bad, right or wrong, just accept them for what they are – just news and keep moving forward without getting too caught up in the highs or lows. Stay focused and remain calm in the face of outside opinions and distractions. If you find yourself in a place where you asking too many people for their thoughts, you probably are abstaining from making a decision yourself.

# 4
## Wipe your mouth and move on.

I developed a simple ritual after every setback: I would "wipe my mouth and move on." This physical gesture became my reset button, my way of acknowledging the fall while refusing to stay down. Success isn't about avoiding falls—it's about getting up one more time than you fall. You will fall down, a lot, so get good at landing safely, or get comfortable with the pain.

# 5
## Pay attention.

Where you focus your energy matters. Be observant, stay curious, and ask thought-provoking questions. Don't hesitate to dig deeper for answers. People will notice when you truly care about something or someone. Pay attention to the details, such as how people dress and smell, or whether they have nice shoes. A fresh haircut or nicely polished nails—these little things make a difference in my opinion. Also, be mindful of how you present yourself: look sharp, smell good, and always treat everyone with kindness and respect, regardless of their status. It's the way you treat every person that gets noticed. I was really disappointed that when Simon Sinek visited my office, he was less than charming to our receptionist.

# 6
## Who you gonna call?

You've just played the game of your life or closed the deal of your dreams—so, who are you going to call? After that significant accomplishment or success, who do you call to share the good news? Who deserves a text, phone call, or voice note to hear your gratitude and love? Take a moment now to thank those who have supported and sacrificed for you along the way. In the midst of preparing for a game, I always remind my players to think about the people who helped get them there. Who drove them across the country? Who believed in them when they didn't believe in themselves? Have we thanked them enough? Let this be your reminder to reach out and show your appreciation. I make it a habit to message the last five people on my WhatsApp list every week—just a simple hello can reignite connections we may not have realised we were missing. One day, I decided to tell my five closest friends that I loved them. Not one of them questioned it; each replied with the same sentiment. The power of gratitude and connection cannot be measured, so why not start now? You don't need a specific reason to reach out and spread love and gratitude.

To be honest, do it now, don't wait for something big or good to happen before reaching out.

# 7
## Not taking enough risk is your greatest risk

Not taking a risk is a certain way to experience regret as you age. While you are young, take whatever risks you can. The bigger, the better. Think bigger; there is no such thing as a bad day, as every day above ground is a good one. As you fill your life with commitments, it is said that it gets harder to take risks; I have disproved this on many occasions. So, keep pushing forward and be brave at whatever age you are. It is never too late to take some risks. As I said before experiment a lot. You don't need to dive in every time, sometimes just dip your toe in and always, always get good advice. Seek out great lawyers and accountants to advise you, don't skimp on having the best team to advise on tax and structures for your setup.

# 8
## Stop buying crap

As you are about to buy something, think for a moment: how many times do I need to wear this for it to feel worth it? Will it keep its value? Am I buying it for myself or to show how cool I am? Am I buying it to keep up with the Joneses? How long will it be before I take it to the dump or try to sell it to get some of my money back? You will be surprised by how much you can save by stopping the habit of buying things to impress others. Add that layer of questioning: why am I buying this? This mindset has prevented me from making many unnecessary purchases. Find a way to simplify your life, I went through a phase of only wearing black t-shirts. It's simple to get going every day.

# 9
## Be healthy

Go to the gym and don't stop. Obviously, the physical benefits are nice, but it is the mental strength it gives you that is important. Your health is your wealth; you cannot go at 100 miles an hour without taking care of your engine. Your brain needs constant stimulation; you need cold and hot therapies to wake your body up. Push yourself—run a marathon once, do a triathlon once, and climb mountains. These experiences all teach you how mentally strong you are, you will learn about stamina and hard work. If you want to be successful, you need plenty of both in your corner. Exercise is an effective form of therapy; it is as necessary as brushing your teeth every day. Learn all about Bio-hacking, start your health journey early. Find someone to fix you before you get sick. You don't need to be sick to get better.

# 10

## Stop allowing your thinking to slow you down

It takes a decade to develop an athlete; they say it takes 20 years for mastery. Thoughts become things, so please think good ones. If you allow your thinking to lead you astray, you will lose. When your thoughts take you off course, snap yourself out of it. I used to give my thoughts a name and remind them that their input was not welcome. Talking to yourself is healthy and serves as a great reminder that you are in control. Thoughts are sometimes nonsense, so its ok to ignore them as well.

---

These simple rules will help you accelerate your growth. This book is here to show you how you can expedite this process we call life. The more you work at it, the quicker the good things will happen. It's simple: take bold risks and don't waste time, money, or resources on things or people that do not matter. Stay as healthy and strong as you can be and fill your mind with positive thoughts. If you want to be successful in business, create systems that are repeatable; that's where value exists.

You don't have to own your own business to achieve what you want; you can find the right companies that will allow you to live your best life, without the risks and challenges of employing people. Have few regrets, and don't allow yourself to have bad days; it annoys everyone, especially the competition. Smile as you go through life and leave everyone you meet better than you found them. I might say this a lot.

# CHAPTER THREE:
## Where have you got to in life?

Tell the truth, not the time. Where are you right now? Are you happy with your situation? Are you happy with your circle? If you are not having fun, what's the point? Are you the brightest candle in the room, and can you outlast the rest? How's your work ethic? Your life is a story you're writing every day. The question is: are you the author, or are you letting others write your chapters? Are you free to think and do as you wish?

These are the questions you should be asking yourself daily; those daily check-ins are so important. Have you shown any gratitude today? You will soon realise that if you are not receiving enough love, thanks, or appreciation, it's because you don't give enough of it yourself. Whatever you feel is missing, start giving that out as much as you can.

Everyone is different. Every person on the planet excels at something; some just haven't figured out what it is yet. I put **yet** at the end of every sentence until I can do or achieve it. I haven't won the league yet; I haven't sold a billion yet.

When you need help, whom are you going to ask? Do you think everyone wants you to fail? When things are going well, everyone wants to be your friend; you soon discover who your real friends are when you are lying on the floor, crying yourself to sleep.

Here are the questions you need to ask to find out where you are right now:

Am I living my truth – do I like what I am doing?

What can I do that I will enjoy doing every day?

What is missing? Who is missing in my life?

Do you have a relationship or merely an arrangement?

Can I sell my dream to someone else? Will they want to come on the journey with me.

Am I prepared to give every living moment to this dream? What are you demonstrating in your current job? And don't make the excuse that working for someone else is not the same. If you cannot show your current boss that you are the best employee out there, you are not ready to run your own star ship. You need to be motivated working for someone else before you embark on the lonely journey of running your own.

Let me be clear: until you have mastered all the skills of business and taken a load of risks on someone else's dime, you are not ready to run your own business. Everyone thinks they can manage a business; I often get to listen to people telling me how to run mine, and sometimes they are right. Listen to the critics.

If you want to run your own business, you can kiss goodbye to many things, including your nice holidays. Life will change; you will be overthinking constantly, putting other people's lives ahead of your own. You will experience borrowing money, being skint, feeling frustrated, having nothing, and borrowing to pay others before yourself. Starting your own venture is the hardest job you will ever do. You will become selfless, not selfish. Your clients will frustrate you, your staff will let you down, and you will question why you gave up a comfortable living for this. This is not the easy option. You will be under a microscope all the time, being judged and criticised no matter what you do. The easy option is working for someone else and letting them bear the stress and worry. However, when it works out, the joy is limitless.

It is a huge decision; it is a life-changing decision. Make it early, before real life gets in the way. There is a Hungarian quote: you cannot sit on two chairs at once. Make your decision, stick to it, and give it everything. Don't compare your new life to the old one; comparison is the thief of joy. Once you make the decision, focus on it with all your energy and keep your fingers crossed, if you last a year – you are about 90% ahead of most start-ups.

# CHAPTER FOUR:
## Life is all about the stories you create.

If you feel life is not worthy of a bestseller, now is the perfect time to change the script. As I get older, I think about how many years I have left—how many summers, winters, and holidays; how many conversations and hugs I will receive. You never know when the last conversation is coming, the last dinner, the last time to say, "I love you." Do you think being 25 means it doesn't matter? You are mistaken. Enjoy every minute; sit down with your grandparents and learn about their lives; learn from their mistakes and experiences. Talk to older people and see what they wish they had done better. Ensure your story is big and ambitious; think about the characters you want to include. Make sure it has a happy ending. Spend time with friends you didn't choose and make time for your brothers, sisters, cousins, and parents. How many places have you explored? Have you seen the wonders of the world? Have you attended major sporting events, big concerts, and gatherings? Have you sat in front of an open fire, dived with dolphins, or eaten at a chef's table? Push yourself to do as many things as you can—the more experiences you have, the more stories you will create. And the more stories you have, the better your life will turn out. Stay in nice hotels, stay in youth hostels, sleep on sofas, and mingle with strangers. Experience beautiful places and visit shantytowns to understand poverty. Do many things for others. Work in homeless shelters; find as many ways as you can to give to others. This doesn't mean simply writing a cheque or giving a homeless person money—that doesn't truly solve anything. Talk to strangers and get out of your comfort zone.

People don't do what's important to them; they do what they care enough about. Your days need to be filled with fascination, curiosity, wonder, gratitude, surrender, and love. Get the mundane things right; never let what you don't have spoil what you do have.

Remember, you only come this way once. All's fair in love and travel—travel makes the world go round, and love makes it a much nicer place. You don't find love; it finds you.

You might not get what you ask for, but you will surely not get what you don't ask for.

# CHAPTER FIVE:
## Mind the way you speak, act, and think.

The key to being alive, awake, and aware is language. I believe we can all smile in the same language. A smile brightens any situation and diffuses every argument. My mantra, which is on the wall in every one of my businesses and woven into the football shirts, is: "Success is driven by belief." I believe, and I speak my beliefs out loud every single day. Belief or faith is what got me to where I wanted to be, much more so than logic.

What you say, how you say it, and your optimistic and bright outlook will lead you to the life you desire. The magic words "Abracadabra" mean, "As I speak, I create." Ludwig Wittgenstein once said, "The limits of my language mean the limits of my world." Why would you want to limit yourself in anything? Allow no limits, no caps. Let nothing stand in your way.

Momentum works both ways; when things are going well, it can continue, but when things are going wrong, momentum can spiral out of control. Please be careful what you say and think; your brain doesn't know the difference between truth, a feeling, or a lie. That's why when you say or think something, it tends to happen. When you think about someone and they suddenly phone or text you, that's the universe working to deliver your messages. Words are powerful; some words have as many as 430 different meanings, so be clear and concise. Ensure that your words, actions, and thoughts are aligned. Think positive thoughts, and positive things will start to happen. In 2012, I told myself that money was like a dripping tap, and only I could switch it off. Consequently, each year, it drips plenty of money towards me; there is always more money, though there is not always more time. You can attract through your language and thoughts. Laugh in stressful situations; laughter can sometimes change the energy in your body. Find the fun in life, and don't let anyone bring you down. A recipe for a calm life is to be neither too high nor too low. Mark Twain famously said, "Kindness is the language which the deaf can hear and the blind can see." Be kind to everyone you meet; you have no idea what they are going through at this moment. If someone is not acting as you expect them to, check in and see where you can help. As you improve, your energy will pick up when others are offline.

I particularly like this quote by Rita Mae Brown: "Language is the road map of a culture. It tells you where its people come from and where they are going." Please don't give off the wrong messages.

Make sure you radiate warmth, allowing everyone you meet to feel comfortable sharing anything with you, and always view life with optimism.

The best people I have met always give everyone a chance to shine. Don't associate with those who bang on about their own lives, who they know, or how much they have done. Self-interested individuals will only ever be interested in themselves.

# CHAPTER SIX:
## Man plans and God laughs

Here's an idea for you: what if the universe gives you everything you want mainly to see if you can handle it? You know right now that you want shiny things, bricks and mortar, investments, a partner, a business—are you even able to manage these? You see, failure is the result of getting what you wanted but being unable to manage it. Success is living in a place of serenity, coping with what you have, always looking for and finding more abundance.

Remember, we come alone and will leave alone. Three score years and ten – that's what it says. Yes, you may go earlier; only the good die young. Who wants to work all their life and then, in their prime, be struck down by illness, a nasty virus, or worse, drop down dead? Enjoy your retirement as you work. Create freedom in your life; take mini-life breaks to enjoy the planet. Do good things and help those in need. Build a school in Africa. Go explore the vast world. Be brave, be bold, and stop making excuses.

Think about the sixty- to seventy-year-olds who were about to embark on a year of cruises and round-the-world trips early in 2020. How many didn't make it out the other end, scarred and scared?

"Man plans and God laughs" isn't just a saying – it's a fundamental truth about life. That's why you should never settle for two weeks in the summer and a couple of weeks at Christmas. You can work from anywhere. You don't need to keep changing jobs to find growth; unless you outgrow your current position, stay there and show loyalty. In the early days, I would have been better off not moving around so much. Find a company that values you and will invest in your growth. Don't ask how many holidays you get; ask how they can improve you and what their development policy is. The more valuable you are, the more holidays you can take. Ask better questions. That's how you get ahead. Inquire about what the ideal employee looks like and what would make their business grow quicker. What do you need to do to get promoted? What does the perfect employee look like?

# CHAPTER SEVEN:
## Good Energy

Feelings are energy – positive or negative – and it's okay to not be okay. The art is not to stay there for too long. How much energy do you have? Can you go longer than most in your room? Can you outlast your competitors? Can you show up again and again without any evidence of success? Oh boy, I could write a book on this subject alone. The more times you bounce forward, the better you will be as a human. You fail when you give up. Don't keep doing the same things; that's just insanity. Repackage, reset, and go again and again until you win.

Let me give you an example:

You are eating healthily, sleeping well, your skin and nails are improving, you exercise daily, yet the scales don't reflect the right evidence. So, you give up and revert to eating badly! Success takes time and leaves clues. Are your clothes looser? Can you go one more hole on your belt? Are you needing haircuts more frequently? These are signs that you are doing the right things, and the sabotage is not worth it.

It's the same in business. Where am I on the leader board? Have I been promoted in six months? Am I receiving positive feedback? Look for progress; it's usually very small, and the better you become, the harder it is to recognise. Are my emails improving? Am I having more meaningful conversations? Am I getting closer to a 'yes' or further away?

Energy is everything, and everything is energy—from the food you eat to the way you speak and think. How do you train to be more energetic? You push yourself to find your limits and break through them. Then, you remove anything from your life that holds you back, including limiting beliefs. You find ways to accomplish things that others marvel at. Set yourself extreme targets; just don't be disappointed if you miss them. No one improves by achieving low targets.

Don't lower your standards. What you care about matters. Avoid petty behaviours; surround yourself with winners and appreciate your time on this planet—you don't know how long it will be. The voices in our heads are not always truthful. In fact, most of the time, they are just trying to keep you safe.

If you spend too much time comparing yourself to past moments (both happy and sad), it can drain your energy. Be less rigid; be flexible, go with the flow, and find the evidence to push harder.

We spent a holiday in Bali, where it rained every day. We had massages each night before bed, a personal trainer every morning, boxed three times a week, had a private chef cook our meals, and enjoyed facials, yoga, and sound therapy. Yet the thing we focused on was the weather rather than appreciating the amazing holiday we were experiencing.

Find yourself, be more of yourself, do more for yourself, and keep filling your life with positive moments. Love yourself, appreciate yourself, grow yourself, teach yourself, be kind to yourself, and do more for you.

A simple mantra I follow is: **do more and get better.**

# CHAPTER EIGHT:
## Who Do You See in the Mirror?

One of my favourite exercises was to hold up a mirror to the people I was working with. I would ask quick-fire questions and observe how quickly people would respond—and in some cases, break down. I noted how well they understood themselves. Some of the questions I posed included:

Who are you? What do you do? It's funny; these are the two questions I ask people when they cold call me. You see, some have an answering machine, while I am a questioning machine. Ninety-five per cent of respondents today cannot answer either of those questions.

Anyway, back to the exercise: Do you allow others to finish their thoughts and stories? Are you compassionate, empathetic, and patient? Do you want others to win? How do you feel when people let you down? Are you often late? Do you struggle to pay attention? Who do you wish would tell you they loved you more? Are you happy? Are you disappointed in yourself? And what does nirvana look like?

I have always seen my role as one that gives people a sense of certainty that can make the impossible possible. Life is imperfect and full of uncertainty.

How do we turn humour into humanity? You still don't have to be sick to get better. And one of my personal favourites: hurt people will always hurt people.

What are your blind spots now? What are you not willing to learn more about, perhaps over-believing what you know? What behaviours are you exhibiting that you don't see, but everyone else seems to notice? What emotions are influencing your system based on calculations your logical brain has crafted?

Are you the right person to give feedback to anyone? How can you ask better questions?

Most of the answers are rooted in fear: fear of failure or even fear of success. If you find yourself asking too many people for their opinions or overthinking the risks, you are abdicating your responsibility to make big moves. I encourage you to think early about your big goals and stop allowing your thoughts to slow you down; after all, 50% of success is just starting.

Your self-doubt is holding you back while someone believes in your potential. Right now, someone is scared of how good you can become. If you have time to stop and complain about things, you are moving too slowly.

This chapter is designed to make you think, to encourage you to ask yourself the right questions, and to prevent you from procrastinating your way through life. It is for you to find the love in what you do and to move forward, no matter the challenges. When you are positive and excited, time tends to fly by; if you loathe what you do, time drags slowly, and you waste so much of the limited time you have on the planet.

# FINAL THOUGHTS

**Let's Strive to make better mistakes in the future.**
Every mistake is an opportunity to learn and grow. As long as we don't repeat the same mistake, it isn't really a mistake at all. In fact, the bigger the problems we face, the more fulfilling our lives can be. We should welcome challenges because they often lead to hidden opportunities. It is important to use language that empowers us rather than makes us feel weak or powerless. The words we use can significantly impact how a situation unfolds, so we must choose them carefully. There is always a solution, and sometimes failing or giving up can actually be the best decision. My personal rule is to aim for seven "no's" before I give up on something—this doesn't apply to romantic pursuits, only business endeavours. One of my most successful deals was preceded by 27 rejections; I never

got a "yes," but I kept pushing until I found a way in. When you desire something deeply enough, you will keep striving until you find the right funding, partner, or customer. It takes patience and perseverance to turn your ideas into reality; even Colonel Sanders didn't start KFC until he was in his 60s and received over 1,009 rejections before finding success. J.K. Rowling was also rejected 12 times before "Harry Potter" was finally published, demonstrating just how much determination and resilience can pay off. If your idea doesn't succeed at first, try repackaging it or rethinking your approach. Sometimes, small changes can lead to significant successes for brands and individuals alike.

Is it true that you become better at anything you practice? Sometimes, you simply become good at practicing. Take big leaps, make some noise, promote yourself, create engaging content, and be bold. If the world needs you and your idea, don't be afraid to share it proudly and confidently with them.

Stop living with a mindset of "don'ts" and start living with a mindset of "do's." The more opportunities you give and receive, the closer you will be to discovering your true purpose. Say yes as much as possible.

Right now, you are the youngest you will ever be again. You are also healthy and committed to becoming a better version of yourself by reading this book. Thank you for that. However, you are also the oldest you have ever been, so stop wasting too much time.

It's time to start believing in your abilities and potential. Get off the train of unhappiness at the first available stop. Don't chase after things; it will only lead to more unhappiness. Instead, believe that luck is on your side (I wear lucky pants every day), hold positive beliefs, and trust that good things will come.

I know many people who are great readers and great film buffs.

## *Be a great doer. And do something that you are proud of.*

You have the commodity that us older generations crave: time. The art of living your second life first involves having the hat trick of life—energy, health, and time. Use them wisely and stop wasting any of them today.

In this book, I've shared as many thoughts as I've learned in my 56 years on this planet. Throughout my professional life, I have always surrounded myself with young people, teaching them to be the best versions of themselves, to live at the highest level of energy, and to not worry about money—there is always more to be made. It's a low-vibrational currency; the more energy you have, the more money you will earn. Appreciate time and use it wisely: read, learn, and grow through travel, discover new places, meet new people, and be curious. Embrace as many moments as you can with excitement.

Don't grow old and start chasing these ideals. And don't get caught up in the lies:

Things will get better—it's not always true; they can actually get a lot worse before they improve. You may think money will solve all your problems—it won't; it will only temporarily suspend them. Furthermore, the phrase "sticks and stones may break my bones" rings false; words can hurt, as can actions.

Stop being lazy. Get off Uber—walk and cycle more; get off Deliveroo and cook your own food.

Don't spend too much time on Instagram or TikTok, don't gamble, and don't engage in anything where one person wins and another has to lose. Focus on finding ways for both parties to win. I suppose owning a football team complicates this idea.

Failure can often result from getting what you wanted but being unable to cope with it. Success lies in being able to live in a place of serenity and manage whatever the universe throws at you. For me, it's going to the cinema in the middle of a workday—I am sad to say I am not yet successful.

Never just accept friends by circumstance—school, colleges, university, sports, or work. Ensure they will help you grow and become a better person.

John Lennon told his teacher that when he grew up, he wanted to be happy. I would advise telling people what you do when they ask: "I want to be happy, and I'm in training." Happiness is a long journey; it requires a great deal of work. Start doing the work as early as you can. Find the things that genuinely make you happy, not just those that give you a dopamine hit.

A good life comes from not breaking promises to yourself. If we lied to our friends the way we lie to ourselves, we would have no friends. Your discipline will deliver every time.

More is said than done; why not reverse that quote and do more than you say you will? I think that's the best way to finish.

## The End

Thank you for reading; I appreciate you being on this journey with me. I finished this book on 31st December 2024. Every year, I write a letter to myself from the future. Over the years so many have written a letter - today people are posting about this habit on LinkedIn. It makes me smile and leaves me a little proud. So many things have come true from these letters.

## Here is my letter to myself.
## Please do check on my progress.

December 31, 2025

Dear Simon,

Wow, what a year its been! As I sit here in London about to watch the New Year's day game versus Barnet in **National League** (yes, we got promoted) and reflect on everything we've accomplished with our brands at Ink and Reach over the past year. I can't help but feel immense pride in the impact we've made, the places we've reached, and the people we've empowered along the way. And lets not forget the huge sums we have raised for multiple charities.

I was at the Amex Stadium in May to see Eastbourne Borough lift their first trophy for a decade. And at the time of writing we are still in the FA Cup and Trophy. Professionally I have been part of a team that has transformed Travel and Live Sport. That's super exciting and rewarding bringing so many along the way.

We've absolutely crushed it in travel. And I mean *crushed* it. Our destinations were nothing short of epic – we›re sent people to places that most only dream about. Antarctica›s frozen wilderness, Dubai, Seychelles, Tokyo›s, played golf at Scotland and Ireland›s wild courses, relaxed on the Maldives› and Mauritius pristine beaches – we›ve basically turned travel fantasies into reality. Who else does that (maybe my son)?

From the mystical landscapes of Cappadocia to the ancient stones of Petra, we didn't just sell ads – we sold experiences that will be etched in people's memories forever. Northern Lights in Iceland? Check. Played Piano in Casablanca (ask your parents)? Nailed it. Philippines raw beauty? We partied there. Fiji's blue waters? Was a magical moment.

And sports? Come on. We were everywhere. Super Bowl in New Orleans, Champions League final, US Open, Club World Cup – we didn't just attend, we *lived* these moments. Maybe we had a cheeky bet or two on the derby as well. (What happens in 2025, stays in 2025, right?)

Every single product we touched turned to gold this year, every team broke records. Our campaigns weren't just successful; they were *transformative*. We found ways to connect brands that the industry is still trying to figure out. Inflight content, storytelling, partnerships – we didn't just set the bar, we *launched* the bar into the stratosphere. We sold more influencer led campaigns across TV and iconic billboards worldwide. Business Traveller became a Youtube and Tiktok sensation.

But here's what made me happy – our people. They didn't just perform; they *dominated*. More sales, more earnings, more everything. And bringing Betsy in with her Premier League sports psychology and Brian Wood with his ability to keep attacking? Genius move. We're not just a company; we're a high-performance machine.

Reach TV? We expanded so far, so fast that other networks are probably still trying to work out what just happened. New partnerships, new channels, fresh content – we're not just keeping up, we're *rewriting* the rulebook. We ended 2024 with the worlds biggest influencer, Khaby Lame, this year we have worked with the biggest names in travel and sport – the Ronaldo Saudi deal was sexy. Mr Lyan was all over Reach and people who might never heard of, made us famous.

2025 wasn't about growth. It was about *impact*. Every deal, every destination, every story – we didn't just participate, we *led*. We inspired. We connected. We showed the world that with bold ideas and an unstoppable team, there are no limits.

As I look towards 2026, I'm buzzing. We're not just businesses – we're platforms for transformation.

Here's to more journeys, more records, and making life absolutely brilliant for everyone we touch.

Cheers and bring on 2026 and a proper FA cup run.

*Simon Leslie*

# As I embark on 2025 I want to thank all these people who are coming on the journey with me.

Adam Murray
Alan Williams
Alex Finney
Alfie Pavey
Alyson Rosen
Andrew Smith
Andy Gibson
Andy Meader
Aurelia Goetz
Auric De Carteret
Benjamin Leslie
Brad Barry
Brayden Johnson
Bruno Silva
Camron Gbadebo
Charlie Gibson
CJ Clarke
Dan Quick
Dave Hudson
David Serra
David Sesay
Delwin Duah
Denise Jaschke

Dominic Odusanya
Ethan Gabriel
Felix Ramirez
Fin Western
Finn Ballard Mcbride
Finn Holter
Finn Holter
Freddie Carter
George Alexander
George Leslie
Hunter Furr
Isaac Pitlado
Jack Clarke
James Alabi
Jayden Davis
Joe Wright
John Bonar
Justin Howard
Kai Innocent
Kim Willams
Liam Cleary
Louis Boyle
Lynn Ashlee

Lynnwood Bibbens
Marie Yeo
Mark Duke
Mark Kubatov
Matt Green
Michael Klass
Moussa Diarra
Nicolo Carfigilo
Ollie Kensdale
Patrick Dunne
Pierce Bird
Robin Phillips

Scott Leslie
Shalini Ramakrishnan
Shannon Dubrow
Sheyi Oyelowo
Siya Ligendza
Steve Rowbotham
Tim Fredd
Tricia Clarke
Will Harley
Yahaya Bamba
Yasser Kasim
Zac Leslie

# ABOUT THE AUTHOR

Simon Leslie co-founded Ink the world's largest travel media company. A serial entrepreneur and is the current owner of Eastbourne Borough Football Club. He has written three other books, which document his professional career. There is No F in Sales, White Belt Thinking and Equanimity. He is a husband and father to four boys and a pug. Learn more at Luckyleslie.com and please feel free to reach out on any social platforms.

Printed in Great Britain
by Amazon